BITCOIN FOR BEGINNERS

Ricardo Dias Marques

CONTENTS

Disclaimers	3
What Are Bitcoins?	4
What Are Digital Currencies And How Do They Work?	7
Bitcoins As An Investment	10
How To Access And Use A Bitcoin Account	13
Getting Started	18
Receiving Bitcoin	19
Sending Bitcoin	20
How to Buy Bitcoin	22
Bitcoin Fractions	22
Bitcoins Mining	23
Conclusion	26

DISCLAIMERS

Your Usage Rights

2020 © - All rights reserved.

You may NOT reproduce this book in any way, it cannot be stored in a retrieval system, or transmitted in any form or by any means, this includes electronic, mechanical, photocopying, recording, scanning, or any other means, without the prior written permission of the publisher.

Disclaimer

The material contained inside this book is for educational and informational purposes only. No responsibility can be taken for any results or outcomes resulting from the use of this material.

While the author has taken every attempt to provide information that is both accurate and effective, the author does not assume any responsibility for the accuracy or use/misuse of this information.

All the information and facts were correct and up to date at the time of writing.

WHAT ARE BITCOINS?

Bitcoins are a type of digital currency that can be created via a free software application and transferred across the Internet without the use of financial institutions or clearinghouses. This means that there is no physical form of this currency; it is not like a U.S. Dollar or a Euro, or even like a piece of gold or silver. You cannot touch bitcoins and be in physical possession of them like you can those aforementioned physical currencies.

The best way for you to understand digital currency is by thinking of it as a code. The strength of the code makes the currency stronger. Cryptography ensures that the code cannot be accessed without proper authorization. This code has never been broken, though many people have tried!

How can Bitcoins be used then? A computer, Smartphone, tablet, or any device with Internet access can easily transfer Bitcoins from one person to another, even in transactions between a user and a business website. The number of bitcoins you have are stored in your "digital wallet," which is similar to screens you see when you use online banking forms to authorize transactions.

When a Bitcoin transaction occurs, the bitcoin miners communicate over a Web-based network and add the transaction to transaction logs that record all Bitcoin transactions.

Peer-to-peer file-sharing technology allows all transactions to be processed and documented. An electronic signature is added, allowing the transaction to be stored on the Bitcoin network. This transaction is free for all to see, though you can use multiple bitcoin accounts and not transfer large amounts of bitcoins to each account in order to help camouflage your activities. This hides your accounts from other Bitcoin users, so they do not know which accounts are yours.

Bitcoin is unlike other currencies because it is decentralized; no one agency (world or national) controls the regulation of it. You may think because Bitcoins are a digital currency that there would be an unlimited supply of them, much like the space on a digital or virtual server.

However, thanks to a schedule planned by Bitcoin itself, there will be 21 million bitcoins in the year 2140. This number will be reached by each update being reduced by half every four years until 2140. At that time, there will be no more Bitcoins mined.

To further ensure that the exact number of 21 million Bitcoins will be in circulation in 2140, each Bitcoin is broken down into eight decimal places, leading to 100 million smaller units being created, known as "Santoshi's." The name is based on the founder of Bitcoin, a software developer named Satoshi Nakamoto. Many people think that this name is a mask and helps to hide the true creator of the software.

When "mining" is mentioned, this means that the free application that creates the Bitcoins is automatically adjusted to ensure that the bitcoins are mined at a predictable and limited rate. There is a certain amount of processing work done by the bitcoin miner, allowing the network to control the exact number of bitcoins being circulated at any one time.

Bitcoins are being accepted at more and more retailers and other online sites throughout the world, changing the way people do business online. For instance, domain registrar Namecheap has become the first major domain name registrar to allow the use of bitcoins as payment for domain name registration, Web hosting, SSL certificates, and WhoisGuard on Namecheap. Coinality.com, a site that launched in September 2013, profiles jobs that pay in digital currencies, including Bitcoins. Bloomberg TV said that Coinality.com is the "Monster.com for jobs that pay in Bitcoin."

As you can see, Bitcoin is gaining more influence in our world today. The creators of Bitcoin believe that as bitcoins become more prominent and more mainstream, a true global economy will start to emerge.

Unlike with physical currencies, Bitcoins and other digital currencies will not be hampered by the limitations and red tape of currencies, exchanges, and regulations. As mentioned above, the creators of Bitcoin planned on bitcoins becoming a part of our future, as bitcoins are to continue flowing into the world until 2140.

As a result, it's likely that more and more companies and organizations will start taking Bitcoins and other digital currencies as payment and using them as payment, thus increasing the presence and influence of digital currencies in our physical world as we continue into the 21st century.

WHAT ARE DIGITAL CURRENCIES AND HOW DO THEY WORK?

Digital currencies are electronic money that aren't denominated by any national currency, nor are produced by any government-endorsed central banks. These currencies are known as "alternative currencies," and thus are sometimes called "altcoins."

Many digital currencies are cryptocurrencies, a type of digital currency that relies on cryptography, as well as a proof-of-work scheme. Essentially, it involves a mathematical process to create the currency at a reasonable rate so that the currency doesn't become too numerous, and thus, lose its value. Bitcoin was the first cryptocurrency, while many others have followed.

The second-most valuable "altcoin" is known as "litecoin." It shares many similar features to bitcoin, but it has a shorter block rate (litecoin's block rate is 2.5 minutes versus bitcoin's 10 minutes). This means that the litecoin can be processed and put into people's digital wallets faster than the bitcoin can. Even though litecoin is cheaper than bitcoin, it is not as popular as Bitcoin, and thus, litecoin is used in fewer places than bitcoin.

The third-most valuable "altcoin" is known as "peercoin." It too is modeled after Bitcoin, but unlike Bitcoin, peercoin has no hard limit on how many peercoins will be mined. The only certainty is that peercoin is designed to eventually hit a target of one percent inflation. That could help the peercoin to last long term as a digital currency.

"Namecoin" is the fourth-most valuable "altcoin." It is very interesting because it is the first prominent iteration of the Bitcoin model to serve a function beyond payments. It is designed to manage information access, as it utilizes all of the same Bitcoin principles to serve as a distributed Domain Name System (DNS). With this unique feature, it may survive on its own-even if Bitcoin fails. There may be further variations of this type of model as well in the future.

"Primecoin" is interesting in its own right because the mining of this digital currency actually contributes to society by implementing scientific proof-of- work. As a result, new blocks of this digital currency are generated every minute, which results in smoother difficulty adjustments and faster transaction times.

One other interesting "altcoin" that is not like Bitcoin and the other digital currencies is "ripple." Ripple has gained much venture capital from Google Ventures, Andreessen Horowitz, Lightspeed Venture, and other venture capitalists. It acts as a decentralized payment system and exchange to complement other currencies, both virtual and physical.

Digital currencies work by mining those currencies on one's computer via a "mining" software that brings about the currency. This is recorded in the respective network to show such new units of the currency exist. These coins can go into a person's digital wallet, then be used to complete transactions. The types of transactions include physical items such as books and video games to digital items such as domain name registration and digital salaries for work performed.

As you can see, there are more digital currencies out there than just Bitcoin, and it seems to be that there will probably be more in the future, both based on current digital currencies and even brand-new ones.

As the world continues to become more "digitized" in terms of the Internet and e-commerce, digital currencies will continue to gain more prominence and use. While replacing physical currencies is probably unlikely, especially in the near future, having more sites accepting digital currencies and conducting transactions using digital currencies is probably likely.

BITCOINS AS AN INVESTMENT

Every day, more and more talk about Bitcoins is occurring, not only as a digital currency, but also as a financial investment. Many people are intrigued by this digital currency, but they also have reservations about it as well. For now, we will discuss how to evaluate bitcoins as an investment.

There are Bitcoin exchanges, just as there are stock market exchanges. As of December 2013, the largest full-trading Bitcoin exchanges that are available to everyone include Bitstamp (based in the United States), BTC-e (based in Bulgaria), and Kraken (based in the United States). The world's largest Bitcoin exchange, BTC China, is based in China, but that exchange only allows exchanges of bitcoins for Chinese Yuan/Renminbi.

In order to open an account with these exchanges, you usually have to link a bank account to your Bitcoin exchange account, as you need to wire transfer the money for bitcoins to use in your account. Credit cards and PayPal are not options [at least not at the time of writing] because the transactions can be reversed very easily, whereas a wire transfer cannot be reversed.

Usually, only bank accounts from that specific exchange's home-based country can be linked to the exchange account (for example, CoinBase, based in the U.S., only allows U.S. bank accounts).

Like the financial stock markets, bitcoins fluctuate in value against real currencies such as the U.S. Dollar, the Euro, the Japanese Yen, and others. One important distinction between Bitcoins and real currencies to this point in Bitcoin's history is the fact that Bitcoin's valuation has been much more volatile than real currencies.

In December 2013, Bitcoin's valuation went from about $675 down to about
$425 within twelve hours, about a 37% drop in valuation. That is virtually unheard of with any real currency (barring something major like The Great Depression or some other major economic event).

The reason that this sharp drop in valuation took place is because the People's Bank of China told third-party payment processors that they should have nothing more to do with Bitcoin exchanges. As a result, Bitcoin kept getting cut off from being supplied by the payment processors; in fact, Bitcoin was cut off by three payment processors inside of a week. Banks have also been told to not deal with Bitcoin any longer.

This event reflects the major concern that most financial experts have about the currency. Many feel it is too volatile as an investment, leading to sharp price spikes and declines that are virtually not seen in other currencies, the equity market, or mutual funds. Most financial experts feel that the digital currency must stabilize in value and not be so prone to such rapid peaks and valleys for it to be taken more seriously as a solid investment.

The problem that many financial experts and institutions have with Bitcoin is that not enough is known about how the currency is mined and how it is "regulated", so that the currency stays on track of having 21 million bitcoins in the year 2140.

While safeguards are in place to keep the currency on that path, there have been attempts to try to disrupt the network and give a few select bitcoin miners the ability to mine as many coins as they wish. There has also been concern that a group of miners could combine together, and work toward their mutual benefit, and to the detriment of everyone else on the network. This would occur by harnessing their mining power to get more coins for themselves and leave little to the rest of the network.

As you can see, there is still some question and doubt on how legitimate of a currency Bitcoin is, including its true valuation. This is likely due to the fact that Bitcoin is the first digital currency, and financial experts are unsure of how to truly evaluate its worth.

More and more companies are starting to accept it as payment, but not enough is known about the mining process and how it can maintain itself to fulfill the promise of 21 million bitcoins in the year 2140. Plus, Bitcoin can be susceptible to wild value peaks and valleys whenever an event associated with the network takes place, such as when Chinese third-party payment processors and banks are told to not deal with Bitcoin exchanges.

It will take more time and a longer track record for Bitcoin to establish the trust of the financial community to where Bitcoin can be seen as a solid investment for most investors.

HOW TO ACCESS AND USE A BITCOIN ACCOUNT

With all the current news regarding finances and the Internet, you are likely wondering how to get set up and use Bitcoin. As we mentioned earlier Bitcoin is the network that is using a digital currency to conduct transactions in many places across the Internet. Unlike a physical currency such as U.S. Dollars and Euros, Bitcoins are "mined" on the Internet, and all transactions take place on the Internet with no physical currency actually changing hands.

So just how do you get access to Bitcoins?

There are two ways in which you can gain bitcoins:

1. You can buy bitcoins from various sources
2. You can mine them yourself

There are two main sources from which you can buy bitcoins: regulated exchanges and from other people who are selling them. You can pay for bitcoins in a variety of ways; most people will use either hard cash or wire transfers. It really depends on where you live and who you are buying them from, as different sellers have different requirements for selling bitcoins to others.

Note that it is virtually impossible to purchase bitcoins via such payment methods as credit cards and PayPal. [though this is something that may change in the future]

This is certainly different from most transactions, as most digital items and a great majority of physical items can be paid via either of these two popular payment methods. The main reason why credit cards and PayPal are not accepted for buying bitcoins is because such transactions using these payment methods can be easily reversed with a call to the credit card company or a press of a button in your PayPal account.

Being that the Bitcoin, itself is a transfer of bits, most governments and agencies will not see this as proof of goods changing hands, and consequently, the bitcoin seller will be out of gaining any money for the transaction. Therefore credit cards and PayPal are largely avoided by exchanges and private sellers when offering Bitcoin payment options.

The other main option to gain bitcoins is to mine them yourself. However, this isn't as easy an option as it may sound. For one thing, you need a Field Programmatic Gate Array (FPGA) or an Application Specific Integrated Circuit (ASIC) to really be able to mine Bitcoins on your own. Even a computer with a graphical processing unit (GPU) would not be able to mine for bitcoins nowadays, because the mathematical process of mining them has become too complex.

You also must factor in the amount of electricity used for the computer or circuit to mine those Bitcoins, as there will be more electricity used than is used by most of your household appliances and items.

Even if you do get the necessary equipment for mining, you'd still have to join a pool of other miners in order to really obtain bitcoins. Thus, while mining bitcoins is an option for some, it's for a relatively small portion of the population and is definitely not for everyone.

When you do get bitcoins via purchasing or mining, you need to have a digital wallet. This is similar to an online bank account.

You have several options:

1. A software wallet stored on the hard drive of your computer
2. An online Web-based service that acts as a digital wallet
3. A paper wallet
4. A mobile wallet for your Smartphone or other mobile device

When you want to send bitcoins to someone else, the transaction takes place between your digital wallet and the other person's digital wallet. When this occurs, everyone on the Bitcoin network knows about the transaction. Plus, the history of a transaction can be traced back to the point where the bitcoins were produced. This is thanks to the public ledger where all Bitcoin mining and transaction are recorded.

As you can see, bitcoins can be acquired either via purchasing from a bitcoin seller or from mining the bitcoins yourself, though the latter option is only practical for a small number of people.

You keep the bitcoins in a digital wallet, either on your own computer or via a Web-based service. When you want to conduct a bitcoin transaction, the transaction takes place between your digital wallet and the digital wallet of the other person.

By knowing how a bitcoin account works and how to use it for funding transactions, you now have the opportunity to utilize the first digital currency in the history of humankind when making purchases on the Internet.

Setting Up Your Bitcoins Wallet

There are several places where you can get a Bitcoin Wallet for the purpose of this eBook we will use one that is easy to set up. You can set up your bitcoin account in two ways:

For Windows, Mac and Linux use: Multibit (or Coinbase).

The Windows version v0.5.16 is compatible with Windows

2000 to Windows 8.1

For your Android Phone or Tablet: https://play.google.com/store/apps/details?id=de.schildbach.wallet

Both are Apps that are lightweight to run on your devices.

Follow the on-screen instructions to download and install your bitcoin wallet.

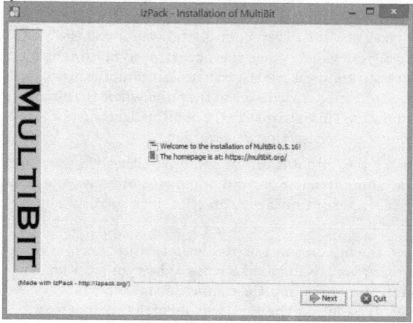

Follow the instructions on the interface to install and set up your Multibit wallet.

BITCOIN FOR BEGINNERS

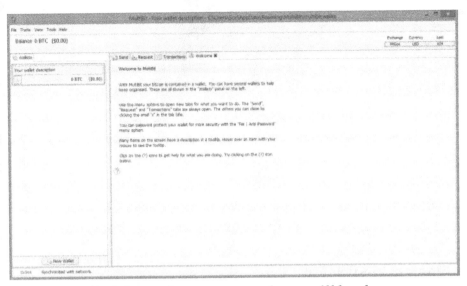

Once installed the Welcome screen above will be shown.

GETTING STARTED

https://multibit.org/en/help/v0.5/help_gettingStarted.html

Your first step is to add a password to your wallet. Adding a password just makes your account more secure but is not mandatory. To create your password, go to:

File - Add Password in the menu options

Your password should be at least 14 characters long, use a password generator such as Lastpass to generate your password for you. Copy your password into a safe place. Without it, you cannot spend your Bitcoin.

You may want to save a copy of your wallet to a USB device as a backup. Make sure you are running a good antivirus software on your computer. If your computer gets hacked your Bitcoin Wallet could be compromised. It is not possible to retrieve your password and if you do lose or forget it, you run the risk of losing all of your bitcoins.

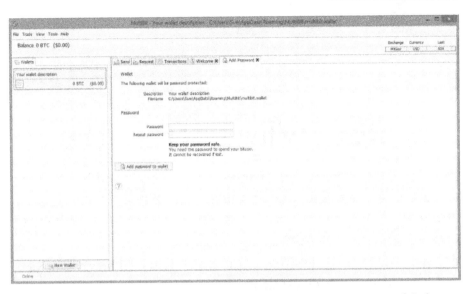

You may wish to set up a 2-step authentication process. This is where an outside source sends you a code to your Smartphone and verifies that you own the account.

RECEIVING BITCOIN

To receive Bitcoin you need to use your Receiving address. This is located in the menu section under Transfers. It is highly recommended that you add a new Receiving address for each new person that you send money to.

The first time you download your wallet you will be given a Receiving address. It looks similar to this:

4Gov7so6kVwTZyP2CDJwKoG5PRThSqf3rr

This is a public address, think of it in the same way as the email address you associate with your PayPal account.

The basic steps to receive Bitcoin are:

1. Create a New Receiving Address - click on the new tab
2. Add a label so you know what the transaction is for
3. Add the amount

Once this happens Multibit will generate a QR code for you. This code contains all of your details. Someone on a mobile device can use this code to send you Bitcoin. You can also copy and paste the code into an email or use to give to a person on Skype.

If you drag the QR code to your desktop it will automatically save as a PNG file for you.

SENDING BITCOIN

To send Bitcoin click on the Send tab.

1. Enter the destination address
2. Enter a label to easily track the payment
3. Add the amount

Once you click Send a pop up will appear to confirm your transaction. This is the only time you can change your mind and cancel it. Once you verify and hit send the transaction is no longer reversible.

When adding the destination address you can type in the address, drag the QR code or copy and paste the code over.

An error message will appear if there was a problem with your transaction. The image below shows what a completed transaction looks like.

Important Note: While anyone can see the buyer's or seller's address, only they can actually unlock the transaction and move the Bitcoin. The unlocking process is accomplished with your private key. Currently each wallet comes with 100 private keys.

Public Key cryptography - means each user has two keys - a series of numbers and letters. One key is public, everyone can see, the other is a private key which only the user has access too. This is important as no matter who sees the transaction it can only be completed by the person with the private key.

HOW TO BUY BITCOIN

Once you have your wallet set up your next step is to buy your Bitcoin. The easiest way to do this is to buy it through an exchange. This works in the same way as any foreign currency exchange.

Some of the top currency exchanges are https://www.bitstamp.net/ https://vip.btcchina.com/ https://local-bitcoins.com/

You can also purchase Bitcoin on sites like eBay, just be aware of their policies as PayPal may not cover these types of purchase under their terms of service, if you should run into an issue with the seller.

As with any purchase also perform your due diligence and research the seller before continuing with any transactions.

Another way to get bitcoins into your wallet is to accept them for payment for something.

BITCOIN FRACTIONS

Bitcoins can be divided into fractions. So, you could technically spend .15 of a Bitcoin on a purchase. The smallest fraction is one hundred millionth of a Bitcoin. This fraction is called a **Satoshi**.

BITCOINS MINING

This currency is being utilized by more and more websites and organizations. As we mentioned earlier, Namecheap, the well-known domain name registrar, just recently started taking Bitcoins as payment.

Other companies are starting to adopt it as well. For bitcoins to be usable, one must first mine them via a computer engaging in a mathematical process to add them to the public ledger that keeps track of all bitcoins on the Bitcoin network. You'll learn more about this process below.

Bitcoin mining involves a software program known as a "bitcoin miner." This program is downloaded onto any device that can connect to the Internet, such as a desktop computer, laptop computer, Smartphone, or tablet.

However, the process is resource-intensive, and even high-end computers with graphical processing units (GPUs) have only a very limited ability to mine Bitcoins. You really need a Field Programmatic Gate Array (FPGA) or an Application Specific Integrated Circuit (ASIC) to really be able to mine bitcoins on your own. If you have either of those, you are in much better shape to mine bitcoins on your own.

The bitcoin miners communicate over the Bitcoin network and verify all legitimate transactions by adding them to a central log, known as the "block chain," that is updated periodically across the entire Bitcoin network. Think public ledger!

The block chain helps to ensure that the total number of bitcoins in circulation at any one time is always known and recorded. The idea behind this is to attempt to keep the value of the Bitcoin currency as stable as possible. When the log is updated, more bitcoins are added to the network as well.

A block chain is a group of transactions which begins with the very first Bitcoin transaction and stops with the latest one. This helps to protect the integrity of Bitcoins and ensures that no fraud or deceptions can take place.

As mentioned above, bitcoin mining is resource intensive. This was designed on purpose to ensure that bitcoins cannot be produced more frequently than what was designed to occur.

This is because there will only be 21 million bitcoins by the time mining ends in 2140. The mining process also has to become more resource intensive as time goes on because already over 50% of the 21 million planned bitcoins have already been mined.

Thus, it will take even longer to mine the remaining bitcoins in the future. Each time a block is mined, an electronic signature is attached and is verified by other bitcoin miners on the network to ensure that those bitcoins are legitimate and can be added to the total number of bitcoins available on the network.

This mining process was established so that no one could control all of the Bitcoin currency, nor could the currency be produced right away. This is in an effort to keep the currency's valuation relatively stable, since there is no physical form in the world and no centralized agency behind the currency.

In addition, by having many bitcoin miners exerting a great deal of computational power to manifest the bitcoins, the miners cannot attack the network itself to where people can take advantage of the Bitcoin network.

Bitcoin is the first digital currency on the Internet, and there have been ramifications both in the digital world and the physical world. In the digital world, more websites and companies are starting to accept it for payment, while other digital currencies are being formed and circulated.

In the physical world, the financial industry and governments around the world are talking more about it and wondering whether to recognize it as a legitimate currency, and if so, how.

Many banks are against digital currencies because they fear the repercussions digital currencies could have on their businesses, businesses that have been stable and dominant for over 100 years. It will be interesting to see how Bitcoin is seen over time as more and more companies, agencies, and individuals use the currency frequently for purchases, transactions, and payments.

Bitcoin Mining can be expensive and is not recommended for everyone. As well as needing the appropriate software, running it can really add up on your hydro bill.
If you would like to become a Miner your best bet is to join a group of Miners. Everyone works together and then shares the profits.

CONCLUSION

One of the easiest ways to get started with using Bitcoins is to sell some of your stuff from home on eBay or Bitify. Why not take the time to do a cleanup and see what items you can sell. This allows you to sell unwanted or unused things that are laying around your home and get some Bitcoins instead.

As you can see there is a lot of technical jargon attached to this cryptocurrency, but once you start to understand the terms, you have a better overall comprehension of what bitcoins are all about.

www.ingramcontent.com/pod-product-compliance
Lightning Source LLC
Chambersburg PA
CBHW032237130525
26658CB00008B/192